BOXER BOOKS Ltd. and the distinctive Boxer Books logo
are trademarks of Union Square & Co., LLC.

Union Square & Co., LLC, is a subsidiary of Sterling Publishing Co., Inc.

This edition first published in North America in 2023. Originally published as
Big Noisy Book of Busy Dinosaurs in 2009.

ISBN 978-1-912757-90-9

Library of Congress Control Number: 2022943978

For information about custom editions, special sales, and premium purchases,
please contact specialsales@unionsquareandco.com.

Printed in China

Lot #:
2 4 6 8 10 9 7 5 3 1

12/22

unionsquareandco.com

The illustrations were prepared using hand-painted paper and digital collage.
The text is set in Futura PT.

A Note from the Author

We know that dinosaurs lived on our planet long ago
because of the fossilized remains they left behind.
Scientists can piece together these fossils to give us an
idea of the shapes of dinosaurs, how they moved, and
even what they ate. However, we can only guess the
colors and patterns of dinosaur skin and imagine
the noises that these creatures made. Today, scientists
study animals like snakes, lizards, and birds to find clues
about how prehistoric animals lived
and what they looked like.

BIG BOOK OF DINOSAURS

Illustrated by
Britta Teckentrup

Written by
Harriet Blackford

Boxer Books

DINOSAURS

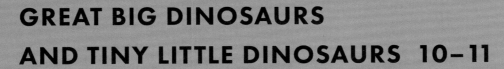

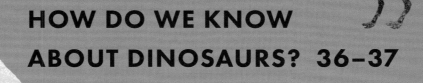

WHAT ARE DINOSAURS?

Dinosaurs are the most famous of all the prehistoric animals. Many were the biggest animals EVER to walk Earth. Dinosaurs were reptiles.

Lizards, crocodiles, snakes, and turtles are all reptiles that exist today.

Some dinosaurs could stand up on their back legs, and some could run really fast on two legs.

The word *dinosaur* means "terrifying lizard." Dinosaurs were around for more than a hundred million years. People have lived on Earth for only two million years! All the dinosaurs died out long before we arrived!

Earth looked very different
when dinosaurs lived here.

There was no ice at the
North or South poles.

There was one big piece
of land, surrounded
by the ocean.

Then the land
broke up into
smaller pieces.

The smaller pieces
looked much more like
the land shapes we
know today.

Dinosaurs came in all shapes and sizes.
Some dinosaurs were vegetarians but
others were fierce, meat-eating hunters!

GREAT BIG DINOSAURS AND TINY LITTLE DINOSAURS

Some dinosaurs were as big as buildings. They had big names, too. Diplodocus was as long as 11 horses standing nose-to-tail in a line.

Brachiosaurus was as tall as three giraffes standing on top of one another. Brachiosaurus could eat off the top of a tree, or just push it over to get the leaves!

It would take 11 elephants to play seesaw with a Brachiosaurus.

Dinosaurs were big, but their brains were small.

Stegosaurus had a body the size of a truck but a brain the size of a ping-pong ball.

You are much smaller than Stegosaurus, but your brain is much bigger.

One of the smallest dinosaurs, Compsognathus, was the size of a turkey.

Eoraptor was about as tall as you are, and it was a fierce little hunter.

ON THE LAND

Gigantic dinosaurs roamed over the land, looking for plants to eat. There were lots of amazing plants—but no grass!

Herds of titanosaurs grazed on plants.

A Diplodocus tail was as long as its neck. Scientists think Diplodocus could thrash its very long tail to make a loud whipping sound.

The big plant-eating dinosaurs had noisy stomachs. They did not chew their food but swallowed stones to help grind up the tons of plants they ate.

Argentinosaurus was so big it had to eat tons and tons of plants each day to keep it from feeling hungry.

Can you imagine the size of Argentinosaurus's poop?

All the dinosaurs stomping around disturbed plants and clouds of insects, which attracted tiny pterosaurs.

HUNTING DINOSAURS

While plant-eating dinosaurs grazed, meat-eating dinosaurs were watching and waiting.

Tyrannosaurus rex was a giant biting machine. T. rex could open its mouth more than a yard wide. Do you think you could fit inside its mouth?

T. rex was tall enough to see into the first floor of a modern-day house. Tyrannosaurus would hide and wait for a big fat dinosaur to come near.

Then T. rex would run out of its hiding place and take a great big bite of its dinner.

Meat-eating dinosaurs swallowed their food in one big bite. T. rex could tear off as much in one bite as 300 steak dinners!

Dromaeosaurs, also known as "raptors," were much smaller hunters than T. rex— about the size of a grown-up person.

A pack of raptors could jump on a big dinosaur and bring it down with their clawed hands and feet.

A T. rex tooth was nearly as long as this page!

Deinonychus had really scary knifelike claws, bigger than your hand, on its back feet. Its name means "terrible claw."

HEAD-BUTTING DINOSAURS

Pachycephalosaurs, sometimes called boneheads, were plant-eating dinosaurs with bony domes on top of their heads. Their name means "thick-headed reptiles."

Pachycephalosaurus was the biggest of the boneheads. Its skull was several inches thick, leaving very little room for a brain!

This one had bumps around the sides of its head.

Some, like Stygimoloch, had horns and spikes sticking out the backs of their heads.

Scientists used to think that the male boneheads would fight by charging at each other and smashing their heads together!

Now scientists think boneheads rammed into the sides of their rivals. This would make their horns and spikes more useful and dangerous.

DINOSAURS WITH HORNS

Ceratopsians were dinosaurs with huge heads, bony neck frills, and horns. Their name means "horned face."

Triceratops was as big as an elephant and had three horns on the front of its head. Around its neck it had a hard, bony neck frill that was difficult for a meat-eating dinosaur to bite.

Styracosaurus had horns around its neck frill.

Pentaceratops
had five horns!

Scientists think male ceratopsians used
their fancy neck frills and horns to show off
to other males at mating time. Maybe their
neck frills were very colorful.
We will never know for sure.

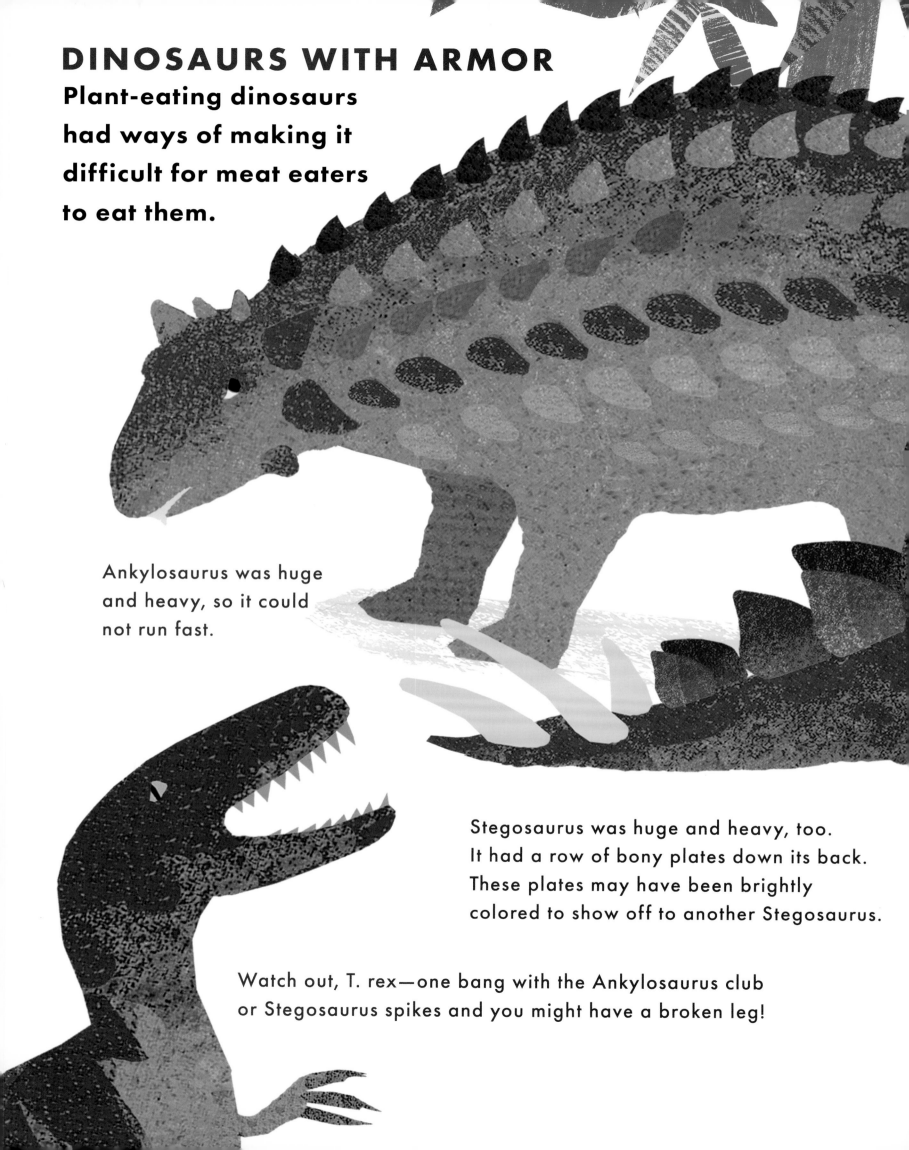

DINOSAURS WITH ARMOR

Plant-eating dinosaurs had ways of making it difficult for meat eaters to eat them.

Ankylosaurus was huge and heavy, so it could not run fast.

Stegosaurus was huge and heavy, too. It had a row of bony plates down its back. These plates may have been brightly colored to show off to another Stegosaurus.

Watch out, T. rex—one bang with the Ankylosaurus club or Stegosaurus spikes and you might have a broken leg!

The body of Ankylosaurus was covered from nose to tail with strong, flat spines. It even had bony eyelid covers! Only its stomach was soft.

Ankylosaurus had a stiff tail with a weapon at the end that looked like a club.

Scientists think Stegosaurus may have used its plates to help it warm up by facing them toward the sun.

FANCY CRESTS

Some dinosaurs, called hadrosaurs, had very fancy head crests. Their crests were hollow.

Scientists think that if one hadrosaur in the herd spotted a meat-eating dinosaur, it could boom loudly to the rest of the herd as a warning.

Hadrosaur crests may have had brightly colored patterns.

Hadrosaurs' mouths were shaped like beaks. This is why they are called duck-billed dinosaurs.

Hadrosaurs could chew on the toughest of plants and grind them down with their hundreds of teeth.

You need cheeks to chew properly; otherwise food falls out of your mouth. Reptiles today do not have cheeks, but some dinosaurs did.

Hadrosaurs were good parents. They looked after their nest full of eggs and cared for their babies.

When they hatched, baby hadrosaurs were the size of chickens.

FEATHERED DINOSAURS

Archaeopteryx was the first fossil of a bird ever found, and its name means "ancient wing."

We do not know what color it was, but this is what we think it might have looked like.

Archaeopteryx had the feathers and wings of a bird but the teeth and the tail of a dinosaur. It was about the size of a crow.

Unenlagia is the most birdlike dinosaur found so far. It could move its arms and shoulders the way a bird moves its wings.

Sinosauropteryx ran on two legs and had sharp teeth to eat meat with.

The back and sides of Sinosauropteryx were covered with feathers to keep it warm.

Velociraptor was a fearsome birdlike dinosaur with long, curved toe claws.

Watch a blackbird run across the grass and think about those fast-running, meat-eating dinosaurs.

UNDER THE SEA

When dinosaurs ruled Earth, monstrous reptiles lived in the sea. These reptiles needed to come up to the surface to breathe. They were not dinosaurs, but they were the best hunters in the water.

Plesiosaurs fished by twisting their very, very long necks and swimming with their flippers.

Placodus had long front teeth to scrape off shellfish from rocks. It ate the meat and spat out the crunched-up shells.

Nothosaurus had webbed feet. Scientists think it may have climbed out of the water to sunbathe on the shore.

Deinosuchus was a giant crocodile that hunted by hiding under the surface of the water, then suddenly grabbing an unsuspecting dinosaur at the water's edge.

The biggest jaws in the world belonged to Liopleurodon. Its mouth was almost 10 feet long!

Ichthyosaurs were dolphin-shaped reptiles. They used their tails to swim fast, and they chased fish and squid to eat.

IN THE AIR

The skies were filled with flying reptiles called pterosaurs.

The tiny Pterodactyl was as small as a sparrow.

This great big one is a Pteranodon.

Pterosaurs were the biggest flying animals that ever lived.

Pterosaurs had thin skin stretched between their fingers and legs to form wings.

Gnathosaurus had teeth that got bigger and longer down the length of its beak.

Some pterosaurs, like Rhamphorynchus, had long beaks to catch fish with.

Others, like Dimorphodon, had short, fat beaks.

Some had fancy crests that may have been very colorful.

Dsungaripterus had a pointy, upturned jaw that may have helped it hunt for creepy-crawlies hiding in cracks in rocks.

Pterodaustro had hundreds of bristles instead of teeth. It swept its head from side to side, catching food in the bristles—just as flamingos do today.

BABY DINOSAURS
Dinosaurs laid oval-shaped eggs of all different sizes.

Some were the size of a soccer balll.

Baby Diplodocus came from an egg the size of a basketball.

Some eggs were the size of a small chicken's egg.

Gigantic mother dinosaurs found somewhere soft to lay their eggs and then covered them with soil, sand, or plants to keep them warm.

Some mothers simply left their eggs. Others, like the duck-billed dinosaur called Maiasaurus, nested in groups and cared for their eggs and babies.

Maiasaurus means "good mother lizard."

Baby dinosaurs had a sharp egg tooth at the end of their beaks to help them chip their way out of the shell.

Scientists think Triceratops may have formed a circle to protect their young with their sharp horns when meat-eating dinosaurs were nearby.

Other animals, especially sneaky little prehistoric mammals, would eat the eggs if they could find them.

MORE GIANTS
Here are some more really big dinosaurs with really big names.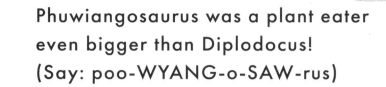

Phuwiangosaurus was a plant eater
even bigger than Diplodocus!
(Say: poo-WYANG-o-SAW-rus)

Mamenchisaurus was a
giant plant eater.
(Say: ma-MENCH-ih-SAW-rus)

Carcharodontosaurus was a
giant meat eater like
Tyrannosaurus rex.
(Say: kar-KAR-oh-DONT-oh-SAW-rus)

Iguanodon was one of the first
dinosaur fossils found.

Models of dinosaurs were made in 1854 and put in a London park. The Iguanodon was so big that a dinner party was held inside its hollow body!

Just like you and me, scientists have to learn. Many fossils were found and studied before scientists knew how dinosaur bones fit together.

We now know Iguanodon had a long spike on its thumb. But at first scientists thought the spike went on the end of its nose.

WHERE DID ALL THE DINOSAURS GO?
Dinosaurs seem to have disappeared 65 million years ago.

Some scientists think that a gigantic, hot meteorite from space crashed into Earth and caused earthquakes, volcanic eruptions, and huge waves in the sea.

Clouds of dust built up in the air and blocked out the sun, making the world cold and dark.

Plants need sunlight to make food. If plants die, the animals that feed on them will die. When the big plant eaters died, the meat eaters that fed on them died, too.

Not all living things died out, of course. The world is still full of beautiful animals and plants, but there are no more dinosaurs!

HOW DO WE KNOW ABOUT DINOSAURS?

When an animal dies, it is often eaten by another animal. Its bones get scattered around. Sometimes animals get covered with layers of sand, dirt, or mud. Over thousands of years, the mud turns to rock. Chemicals in the rocks change the bones to stone. Then we have a fossil.

When scientists find a fossil, they dig around it very carefully, chipping away at the rock with little hammers and brushing away the dust.

Each fossil piece found is mapped on a plan of the dig site and then it is labeled.

Scientists try to fit the pieces together to see what the living animal might have looked like.

It's not just bones that make fossils. Dinosaur eggs have been found with fossilized babies inside them.

Fossils of dinosaur poop called coprolites tell scientists what dinosaurs ate.

Footprints made by a group of Apatosaurus have been found in the United States.

Smaller footprints were found there, too, making scientists think that Apatosaurus must have traveled in groups with their young.